The Poetry Of Amy Levy

Amy Levy was born in London, Eng
fairly wealthy Anglo-Jewish family.
participated in secular literary activit
Victorian life.

Amy was educated at Brighton High Sc   ᴜᴅied at
Newnham College, Cambridge; she was   ...ᴠʜ student when she
arrived in 1879, but left after four terms

But her writing career was to begin early; her poem "Ida Grey" appearing
when she was only fourteen. Her stories "Cohen of Trinity" and "Wise in
Their Generation," were published by Oscar Wilde in his magazine
"Women's World," and are considered among her best.

Her first novel Romance of a Shop, written in 1888 is based on four
sisters who experience the pleasures and hardships of running a business
in London during the 1880s. This was followed by Reuben Sachs (also
1888) and concerned with Jewish identity and mores in the England of her
time and therefore somewhat controversial);

Her other writings reveal feminist concerns; Xantippe and Other Verses,
from 1881 includes a poem in the voice of Socrates's wife; the volume A
Minor Poet and Other Verse from 1884 has dramatic monologues and lyric
poems.

In 1886, Levy began a series of essays on Jewish culture and literature
for the Jewish Chronicle, including The Ghetto at Florence, The Jew in
Fiction, Jewish Humour and Jewish Children.

That same year while travelling in Florence she met writer Vernon Lee. It
is generally assumed they fell in love and this inspired the poem 'To
Vernon Lee'.

Her final book of poems, A London Plane-Tree from 1889, shows the
beginnings of the influence of French symbolism.

Despite many friendships and active life, Amy had suffered for a long time
with major depression and this, together with her growing deafness, led
her to commit suicide by inhaling carbon monoxide on September 10,
1889, at the age of twenty-seven.

Index Of Poems

To Vernon Lee
On Bellosguardo, when the year was young,
We wandered, seeking for the daffodil
And dark anemone, whose purples fill
The peasant's plot, between the corn-shoots sprung.

Over the grey, low wall the olive flung
Her deeper greyness ; far off, hill on hill
Sloped to the sky, which, pearly-pale and still,
Above the large and luminous landscape hung.

A snowy blackthorn flowered beyond my reach;
You broke a branch and gave it to me there;
I found for you a scarlet blossom rare.

Thereby ran on of Art and Life our speech;
And of the gifts the gods had given to each
Hope unto you, and unto me Despair.

Youth and Love

What does youth know of love?
Little enough, I trow!
He plucks the myrtle for his brow,
For his forehead the rose.
Nay, but of love
It is not youth who knows.

A March Day in London
The east wind blows in the street to-day;
The sky is blue, yet the town looks grey.
'Tis the wind of ice, the wind of fire,
Of cold despair and of hot desire,
Which chills the flesh to aches and pains,
And sends a fever through all the veins.

From end to end, with aimless feet,
All day long have I paced the street.
My limbs are weary, but in my breast
Stirs the goad of a mad unrest.
I would give anything to stay
The little wheel that turns in my brain;
The little wheel that turns all day,
That turns all night with might and main.

What is the thing I fear, and why?
Nay, but the world is all awry
The wind's in the east, the sun's in the sky.
The gas-lamps gleam in a golden line;
The ruby lights of the hansoms shine,
Glance, and flicker like fire-flies bright;
The wind has fallen with the night,
And once again the town seems fair
Thwart the mist that hangs i' the air.

And o'er, at last, my spirit steals
A weary peace; peace that conceals
Within its inner depths the grain
Of hopes that yet shall flower again.

Borderland
Am I waking, am I sleeping?
As the first faint dawn comes creeping
Thro' the pane, I am aware
Of an unseen presence hovering,
Round, above, in the dusky air:

A downy bird, with an odorous wing,
That fans my forehead, and sheds perfume,
As sweet as love, as soft as death,
Drowsy-slow through the summer-gloom.
My heart in some dream-rapture saith,
It is she. Half in a swoon,
I spread my arms in slow delight.
O prolong, prolong the night,
For the nights are short in June!

A London Plane-Tree
Green is the plane-tree in the square,
The other trees are brown;
They droop and pine for country air;
The plane-tree loves the town.

Here from my garret-pane, I mark
The plane-tree bud and blow,
Shed her recuperative bark,
And spread her shade below.

Among her branches, in and out,
The city breezes play;
The dun fog wraps her round about;
Above, the smoke curls grey.

Others the country take for choice,
And hold the town in scorn;
But she has listened to the voice
On city breezes borne.

The Birch-Tree at Loschwitz
At Loschwitz above the city
The air is sunny and chill;
The birch-trees and the pine-trees
Grow thick upon the hill.

Lone and tall, with silver stem,
A birch-tree stands apart;
The passionate wind of spring-time
Stirs in its leafy heart.

I lean against the birch-tree,
My arms around it twine;
It pulses, and leaps, and quivers,

Like a human heart to mine.

One moment I stand, then sudden
Let loose mine arms that cling:
O God! the lonely hillside,
The passionate wind of spring!

Philosophy
Ere all the world had grown so drear,
When I was young and you were here,
'Mid summer roses in summer weather,
What pleasant times we've had together!

We were not Phyllis, simple-sweet,
And Corydon; we did not meet
By brook or meadow, but among
A Philistine and flippant throng

Which much we scorned; (less rigorous
It had no scorn at all for us!)
How many an eve of sweet July,
Heedless of Mrs. Grundy's eye,

We've scaled the stairway's topmost height,
And sat there talking half the night;
And, gazing on the crowd below,
Thanked Fate and Heaven that made us so;

To hold the pure delights of brain
Above light loves and sweet champagne.
For, you and I, we did eschew
The egoistic "I" and "you;"

And all our observations ran
On Art and Letters, Life and Man.
Proudly we sat, we two, on high,
Throned in our Objectivity;

Scarce friends, not lovers (each avers),
But sexless, safe Philosophers.

* * * * * *
Dear Friend, you must not deem me light
If, as I lie and muse to-night,
I give a smile and not a sigh
To thoughts of our Philosophy.

In September

The sky is silver-grey; the long
Slow waves caress the shore.
On such a day as this I have been glad,
Who shall be glad no more.

New Love, New Life

I.

She, who so long has lain
Stone-stiff with folded wings,
Within my heart again
The brown bird wakes and sings.

Brown nightingale, whose strain
Is heard by day, by night,
She sings of joy and pain,
Of sorrow and delight.

II.

'Tis true, in other days
Have I unbarred the door;
He knows the walks and ways
Love has been here before.

Love blest and love accurst
Was here in days long past;
This time is not the first,
But this time is the last.

Ralph to Mary

Love, you have led me to the strand,
Here, where the stilly, sunset sea,
Ever receding silently,
Lays bare a shining stretch of sand;

Which, as we tread, in waving line,
Sinks softly 'neath our moving feet;
And looking down our glances meet,
Two mirrored figures, yours and mine.

To-night you found me sad, alone,
Amid the noisy, empty books

And drew me forth with those sweet looks,
And gentle ways which are your own.

The glory of the setting sun
Has sway'd and softened all my mood;
This wayward heart you understood,
Dear love, as you have always done.

Have you forgot the poet wild,
Who sang rebellious songs and hurl'd
His fierce anathemas at 'the world,'
Which shrugg'd its shoulders, pass'd and smil'd?

Who fled in wrath to distant lands,
And sitting, thron'd upon a steep,
Made music to the mighty deep,
And thought, 'Perhaps it understands.'

Who back return'd, a wanderer drear,
Urged by the spirit's restless pain,
Sang his wild melodies in vain
Sang them to ears that would not hear. . .

A weary, lonely thing he flies,
His soul's fire with soul's hunger quell'd,
Till, sudden turning, he beheld
His meaning, mirrored in your eyes! . . .

Ah, Love, since then have passed away
Long years ; some things are chang'd on earth;
Men say that poet had his worth,
And twine for him the tardy bay.

What care I, so that hand in hand,
And heart in heart we pace the shore?
My heart desireth nothing more,
We understand, we understand.

The Piano-Organ
My student-lamp is lighted,
The books and papers are spread;
A sound comes floating upwards,
Chasing the thoughts from my head.

I open the garret window,
Let the music in and the moon;

See the woman grin for coppers,
While the man grinds out the tune.

Grind me a dirge or a requiem,
Or a funeral-march sad and slow,
But not, O not, that waltz tune
I heard so long ago.

I stand upright by the window,
The moonlight streams in wan:
O God! with its changeless rise and fall
The tune twirls on and on.

Oh, Is It Love?
O is it Love or is it Fame,
This thing for which I sigh?
Or has it then no earthly name
For men to call it by?

I know not what can ease my pains,
Nor what it is I wish;
The passion at my heart-strings strains
Like a tiger in a leash.

The Dream
A fair dream to my chamber flew:
Such a crowd of folk that stirred,
Jested, fluttered; only you,
You alone of all that band,
Calm and silent, spake no word.
Only once you neared my place,
And your hand one moment's space
Sought the fingers of my hand;
Your eyes flashed to mine; I knew
All was well between us two.

* * * * *

On from dream to dream I past,
But the first sweet vision cast
Mystic radiance o'er the last.

* * * * *

When I woke the pale night lay

Still, expectant of the day;
All about the chamber hung
Tender shade of twilight gloom;
The fair dream hovered round me, clung
To my thought like faint perfume:
Like sweet odours, such as cling
To the void flask, which erst encloses
Attar of rose; or the pale string
Of amber which has lain with roses.

Cambridge in the Long

Where drowsy sound of college-chimes
Across the air is blown,
And drowsy fragrance of the limes,
I lie and dream alone.

A dazzling radiance reigns o'er all
O'er gardens densely green,
O'er old grey bridges and the small,
Slow flood which slides between.

This is the place; it is not strange,
But known of old and dear.
What went I forth to seek? The change
Is mine; why am I here?

Alas, in vain I turned away,
I fled the town in vain;
The strenuous life of yesterday
Calleth me back again.

And was it peace I came to seek?
Yet here, where memories throng,
Ev'n here, I know the past is weak,
I know the present strong.

This drowsy fragrance, silent heat,
Suit not my present mind,
Whose eager thought goes out to meet
The life it left behind.

Spirit with sky to change; such hope,
An idle one we know;
Unship the oars, make loose the rope,
Push off the boat and go. . .

Ah, would what binds me could have been
Thus loosened at a touch!
This pain of living is too keen,
Of loving, is too much.

Out of Town

Out of town the sky was bright and blue,
Never fog-cloud, lowering, thick, was seen to frown;
Nature dons a garb of gayer hue,
Out of town.

Spotless lay the snow on field and down,
Pure and keen the air above it blew;
All wore peace and beauty for a crown.

London sky, marred by smoke, veiled from view,
London snow, trodden thin, dingy brown,
Whence that strange unrest at thoughts of you
Out of town?

In the Black Forest

I lay beneath the pine trees,
And looked aloft, where, through
The dusky, clustered tree-tops,
Gleamed rent, gay rifts of blue.

I shut my eyes, and a fancy
Fluttered my sense around:
"I lie here dead and buried,
And this is churchyard ground.

"I am at rest for ever;
Ended the stress and strife."
Straight I fell to and sorrowed
For the pitiful past life.

Right wronged, and knowledge wasted;
Wise labour spurned for ease;
The sloth and the sin and the failure;
Did I grow sad for these?

They had made me sad so often;
Not now they made me sad;
My heart was full of sorrow
For joy it never had.

On the Threshold

O God, my dream! I dreamed that you were dead;
Your mother hung above the couch and wept
Whereon you lay all white, and garlanded
With blooms of waxen whiteness. I had crept
Up to your chamber-door, which stood ajar,
And in the doorway watched you from afar,
Nor dared advance to kiss your lips and brow.
I had no part nor lot in you, as now;
Death had not broken between us the old bar;
Nor torn from out my heart the old, cold sense
Of your misprision and my impotence.

On the Wye in May

Now is the perfect moment of the year.
Half naked branches, half a mist of green,
Vivid and delicate the slopes appear;
The cool, soft air is neither fierce nor keen,

And in the temperate sun we feel no fear;
Of all the hours which shall be and have been,
It is the briefest as it is most dear,
It is the dearest as the shortest seen.

O it was best, belovèd, at the first.
Our hands met gently, and our meeting sight
Was steady; on our senses scarce had burst
The faint, fresh fragrance of the new delight. . .

I seek that clime, unknown, without a name,
Where first and best and last shall be the same.

June

Last June I saw your face three times;
Three times I touched your hand;
Now, as before, May month is o'er,
And June is in the land.

O many Junes shall come and go,
Flow'r-footed o'er the mead;
O many Junes for me, to whom
Is length of days decreed.

There shall be sunlight, scent of rose;
Warm mist of summer rain;
Only this change, I shall not look
Upon your face again.

A June-Tide Echo

In the long, sad time, when the sky was grey,
And the keen blast blew through the city drear,
When delight had fled from the night and the day,
My chill heart whispered, " June will be here!

" June with its roses a-sway in the sun,
Its glory of green on mead and tree."
Lo, now the sweet June-tide is nearly done,
June-tide, and never a joy for me

Is it so much of the gods that I pray?
Sure craved man never so slight a boon!
To be glad and glad in my heart one day
One perfect day of the perfect June.

Sweet sounds to-night rose up, wave upon wave;
Sweet dreams were afloat in the balmy air.
This is the boon of the gods that I crave
To be glad, as the music and night were fair.

For once, for one fleeting hour, to hold
The fair shape the music that rose and fell
Revealed and concealed like a veiling fold;
To catch for an instant the sweet June spell.

For once, for one hour, to catch and keep
The sweet June secret that mocks my heart;
Now lurking calm, like a thing asleep,
Now hither and thither with start and dart.

Then the sick, slow grief of the weary years,
The slow, sick grief and the sudden pain;
The long days of labour, the nights of tears
No more these things would I hold in vain.

I would hold my life as a thing of worth;
Pour praise to the gods for a precious thing.
Lo, June in her fairness is on earth,
And never a joy does the niggard bring.

London in July

What ails my senses thus to cheat?
What is it ails the place,
That all the people in the street
Should wear one woman's face?

The London trees are dusty-brown
Beneath the summer sky;
My love, she dwells in London town,
Nor leaves it in July.

O various and intricate maze,
Wide waste of square and street;
Where, missing through unnumbered days,
We twain at last may meet!

And who cries out on crowd and mart?
Who prates of stream and sea?
The summer in the city's heart
That is enough for me.

The Sequel to a Reminiscence

Not in the street and not in the square,
The street and square where you went and came;
With shuttered casement your house stands bare,
Men hush their voice when they speak your name.

I, too, can play at the vain pretence,
Can feign you dead; while a voice sounds clear
In the inmost depths of my heart: Go hence,
Go, find your friend who is far from here.

Not here, but somewhere where I can reach!
Can a man with motion, hearing and sight,
And a thought that answered my thought and speech,
Be utterly lost and vanished quite?

Whose hand was warm in my hand last week?
My heart beat fast as I neared the gate
Was it this I had come to seek,
"A stone that stared with your name and date;"

A hideous, turfless, fresh-made mound;
A silence more cold than the wind that blew?
What had I lost, and what had I found?

My flowers that mocked me fell to the ground
Then, and then only, my spirit knew.

Captivity
The lion remembers the forest,
The lion in chains;
To the bird that is captive a vision
Of woodland remains.

One strains with his strength at the fetter,
In impotent rage;
One flutters in flights of a moment,
And beats at the cage.

If the lion were loosed from the fetter,
To wander again;
He would seek the wide silence and shadow
Of his jungle in vain.

He would rage in his fury, destroying;
Let him rage, let him roam!
Shall he traverse the pitiless mountain,
Or swim through the foam?

If they opened the cage and the casement,
And the bird flew away;
He would come back at evening, heartbroken,
A captive for aye.

Would come if his kindred had spared him,
Free birds from afar
There was wrought what is stronger than iron
In fetter and bar.

I cannot remember my country,
The land whence I came;
Whence they brought me and chained me and made me
Nor wild thing nor tame.

This only I know of my country,
This only repeat :
It was free as the forest, and sweeter
Than woodland retreat.

When the chain shall at last be broken,
The window set wide;

And I step in the largeness and freedom
Of sunlight outside ;

Shall I wander in vain for my country?
Shall I seek and not find?
Shall I cry for the bars that encage me
The fetters that bind?

London Poets
(In Memoriam.)

They trod the streets and squares where now I tread,
With weary hearts, a little while ago;
When, thin and grey, the melancholy snow
Clung to the leafless branches overhead;
Or when the smoke-veiled sky grew stormy-red
In autumn; with a re-arisen woe
Wrestled, what time the passionate spring winds blow;
And paced scorched stones in summer: they are dead.

The sorrow of their souls to them did seem
As real as mine to me, as permanent.
To-day, it is the shadow of a dream,
The half-forgotten breath of breezes spent.
So shall another soothe his woe supreme
"No more he comes, who this way came and went."

A Game of Lawn Tennis
What wonder that I should be dreaming
Out here in the garden to-day?
The light through the leaves is streaming,
Paulina cries, "Play!"

The birds to each other are calling,
The freshly-cut grasses smell sweet;
To Teddy's dismay, comes falling
The ball at my feet.

"Your stroke should be over, not under!"
"But that's such a difficult way!"
The place is a springtide wonder
Of lilac and may;

Of lilac, and may, and laburnum,
Of blossom, We're losing the set!

"Those volleys of Jenny's, return them;
"Stand close to the net!"

* * * * * * *

You are so fond of the Maytime,
My friend, far away;
Small wonder that I should be dreaming
Of you in the garden to-day.

A Farewell
The sad rain falls from Heaven,
A sad bird pipes and sings ;
I am sitting here at my window
And watching the spires of "King's."

O fairest of all fair places,
Sweetest of all sweet towns!
With the birds, and the greyness and greenness,
And the men in caps and gowns.

All they that dwell within thee,
To leave are ever loth,
For one man gets friends, and another
Gets honour, and one gets both.

The sad rain falls from Heaven;
My heart is great with woe
I have neither a friend nor honour,
Yet I am sorry to go.

The Sick Man and the Nightingale
So late, and yet a nightingale?
Long since have dropp'd the blossoms pale,
The summer fields are ripening,
And yet a sound of spring?

O tell me, didst thou come to hear,
Sweet Spring, that I should die this year;
And call'st across from the far shore
To me one greeting more?

The First Extra
A Waltz Song.

O sway, and swing, and sway,
And swing, and sway, and swing!
Ah me, what bliss like unto this,
Can days and daylight bring?

A rose beneath your feet
Has fallen from my head;
Its odour rises sweet,
All crushed it lies, and dead.

O Love is like a rose,
Fair-hued, of fragrant breath;
A tender flow'r that lives an hour,
And is most sweet in death.

O swing, and sway, and swing,
And rise, and sink, and fall!
There is no bliss like unto this,
This is the best of all.

The Old House

In through the porch and up the silent stair;
Little is changed, I know so well the ways;
Here, the dead came to meet me; it was there
The dream was dreamed in unforgotten days.

But who is this that hurries on before,
A flitting shade the brooding shades among?
She turned, I saw her face, O God, it wore
The face I used to wear when I was young!

I thought my spirit and my heart were tamed
To deadness; dead the pangs that agonise.
The old grief springs to choke me, I am shamed
Before that little ghost with eager eyes.

O turn away, let her not see, not know!
How should she bear it, how should understand?
O hasten down the stairway, haste and go,
And leave her dreaming in the silent land.

To Sylvia

"O love, lean thou thy cheek to mine,
And let the tears together flow"
Such was the song you sang to me

Once, long ago.

Such was the song you sang; and yet
(O be not wroth!) I scarcely knew
What sounds flow'd forth; I only felt
That you were you.

I scarcely knew your hair was gold,
Nor of the heavens' own blue your eyes.
Sylvia and song, divinely mixt,
Made Paradise.

These things I scarcely knew; to-day,
When love is lost and hope is fled,
The song you sang so long ago
Rings in my head.

Clear comes each note and true; to-day,
As in a picture I behold
Your tur'd-up chin, and small, sweet head
Misty with gold.

I see how your dear eyes grew deep,
How your lithe body thrilled and swayed,
And how were whiter than the keys
Your hands that played. . .

Ah, sweetest! cruel have you been,
And robbed my life of many things.
I will not chide; ere this I knew
That Love had wings.

You've robbed my life of many things
Of love and hope, of fame and pow'r.
So be it, sweet. You cannot steal
One golden hour.

To Lallie (Outside the British Museum.)
Up those Museum steps you came,
And straightway all my blood was flame,
O Lallie, Lallie !
The world (I had been feeling low)
In one short moment's space did grow
A happy valley.
There was a friend, my friend, with you;
A meagre dame in peacock blue

Apparelled quaintly:
This poet-heart went pit-a-pat;
I bowed and smiled and raised my hat;
You nodded faintly.
My heart was full as full could be;
You had not got a word for me,
Not one short greeting;
That nonchalant small nod you gave
(The tyrant's motion to the slave)
Sole mark'd our meeting.
Is it so long ? Do you forget
That first and last time that we met?
The time was summer.
The trees were green; the sky was blue;
Our host presented me to you
A tardy comer.
You look'd demure, but when you spoke
You made a little, funny joke,
Yet half pathetic.
Your gown was grey, I recollect,
I think you patronized the sect
They call "æsthetic."
I brought you strawberries and cream,
And plied you long about a stream
With duckweed laden ;
We solemnly discussed the heat.
I found you shy and very sweet,
A rosebud maiden.
Ah me, to-day! You passed inside
To where the marble gods abide:
Hermes, Apollo,
Sweet Aphrodite, Pan; and where,
For aye reclined, a headless fair
Beats all fairs hollow.
And I, I went upon my way,
Well rather sadder, let us say;
The world looked flatter.
I had been sad enough before,
A little less, a little more,
What does it matter?

Translated from Geibel
O say, thou wild, thou oft deceived heart,
What mean these noisy throbbings in my breast?
After thy long, unutterable woe
Wouldst thou not rest?

Fall'n from Life's tree the sweet rose-blossom lies,
And fragrant youth has fled. What made to seem
This earth as fair to thee as Paradise,
Was all a dream.

The blossom fell, the thorn was left to me;
Deep from the wound the blood-drops ever flow,
All that I have are yearnings, wild desires,
And wrath and woe.

They brought me Lethe's water, saying, 'Drink!'
'Drink, for the draught is sweet,' I heard them say,
'Shalt learn how soft a thing forgetting is.'
I answered : 'Nay.'

What tho' indeed it were an idle cheat,
Nathless to me 'twas very fair and blest:
With every breath I draw I know that love
Reigns in my breast.

Let me go forth, and thou, my heart, bleed on:
A lonely spot I seek by night and day,
That love and sorrow I may there breathe forth
In a last lay.

Christopher Found
I.
At last; so this is you, my dear!
How should I guess to find you here?
So long, so long, I sought in vain
In many cities, many lands,
With straining eyes and groping hands;
The people marvelled at my pain.
They said: "But sure, the woman's mad;
What ails her, we should like to know,
That she should be so wan and sad,
And silent through the revels go?"
They clacked with such a sorry stir!
Was I to tell? were they to know
That I had lost you, Christopher?
Will you forgive me for one thing?
Whiles, when a stranger came my way,
My heart would beat and I would say :
" Here's Christopher!" then lingering
With longer gaze, would turn away

Cold, sick at heart. My dear, I know
You will forgive me for this thing.
It is so very long ago
Since I have seen your face till now;
Now that I see it, lip and brow,
Eyes, nostril, chin, alive and clear;
Last time was long ago; I know
This thing you will forgive me, dear.

II.

There is no Heaven. This is the best;
O hold me closer to your breast;
Let your face lean upon my face,
That there no longer shall be space
Between our lips, between our eyes.
I feel your bosom's fall and rise.
O hold me near and yet more near;
Ah sweet ; I wonder do you know
How lone and cold, how sad and drear,
Was I a little while ago;
Sick of the stress, the strife, the stir;
But I have found you, Christopher.

III.

If only you had come before!
(This is the thing I most deplore)
A seemlier woman you had found,
More calm, by courtesies more bound,
Less quick to greet you, more subdued
Of appetite; of slower mood.
But ah! you come so late, so late!
This time of day I can't pretend
With slight, sweet things to satiate
The hunger-cravings. Nay, my friend,
I cannot blush and turn and tremble,
Wax loth as younger maidens do.
Ah, Christopher, with you, with you,
You would not wish me to dissemble?

IV.

So long have all the days been meagre,
With empty platter, empty cup,
No meats nor sweets to do me pleasure,
That if I crave is it over-eager,
The deepest draught, the fullest measure,
The beaker to the brim poured up?

V.

Shelley, that sprite from the spheres above,
Says, and would make the matter clear,
That love divided is larger love;
We'll leave those things to the bards, my dear.
For you never wrote a verse, you see;
And I my verse is not fair nor new.
Till the world be dead, you shall love but me,
Till the stars have ceased, I shall love but you.

EPILOGUE.

Thus ran the words; or rather, thus did run
Their purport. Idly seeking in the chest
(You see it yonder), I had found them there:
Some blotted sheets of paper in a case,
With a woman's name writ on it: "Adelaide."
Twice on the writing there was scored the date
Of ten years back; and where the words had end
Was left a space, a dash, a half-writ word,
As tho' the writer minded, presently
The matter to pursue.
I questioned her,
That worthy, worthy soul, my châtelaine,
Who, nothing loth, made answer.
There had been
Another lodger ere I had the rooms,
Three months gone by a woman.
"Young, sir? No.
Must have seen forty if she'd seen a day!
A lonesome woman; hadn't many friends;
Wrote books, I think, and things for newspapers.
Short in her temper, eyes would flash and flame
At times, till I was frightened. Paid her rent
Most regular, like a lady.
Ten years back,
They say (at least Ann Brown says), ten years back
The lady had a lover. Even then
She must have been no chicken.
Three months since
She died. Well, well, the Lord is kind and just.
I did my best to tend her, yet indeed
It's bad for trade to have a lodger die.
Her brother came, a week before she died:
Buried her, took her things, threw in the fire
The littered heaps of paper.
Yes, the sheets,

They must have been forgotten in the chest;
I never knew her name was Adelaide."

The Two Terrors
Two terrors fright my soul by night and day:
The first is Life, and with her come the years;
A weary, winding train of maidens they,
With forward-fronting eyes, too sad for tears;
Upon whose kindred faces, blank and grey,
The shadow of a kindred woe appears.
Death is the second terror; who shall say
What form beneath the shrouding mantle nears?

Which way she turn, my soul finds no relief,
My smitten soul may not be comforted;
Alternately she swings from grief to grief,
And, poised between them, sways from dread to dread.
For there she dreads because she knows; and here,
Because she knows not, only faints with fear.

The Lost Friend
I know the face of sorrow, and I know
Her voice with all its varied cadences;
Which way she turns and treads; how at her ease
Things fit her dreary largess to bestow.

Where sorrow long abides, some be that grow
To hold her dear, but I am not of these;
Joy is my friend, not sorrow; by strange seas,
In some far land we wandered, long ago.

O faith, long tried, that knows no faltering!
O vanished treasure of her hands and face!
Beloved to whose memory I cling,
Unmoved within my heart she holds her place.

And never shall I hail that other "friend,"
Who yet shall dog my footsteps to the end.

A Dirge
There's May amid the meadows,
There's May amid the trees;
Her May-time note the cuckoo
Sends forth upon the breeze.

Above the rippling river
May swallows skim and dart;
November and December
Keep watch within my heart.

The spring breathes in the breezes,
The woods with wood-notes ring,
And all the budding hedgerows
Are fragrant of the spring.

In secret, silent places
The live green things upstart;
Ice-bound, ice-crown'd dwells winter
For ever in my heart.

Upon the bridge I linger,
Near where the lime-trees grow;
Above, swart birds are circling,
Beneath, the stream runs slow.

A stripling and a maiden
Come wand'ring up the way;
His eyes are glad with springtime,
Her face is fair with May.

Of warmth the sun and sweetness
All nature takes a part;
The ice of all the ages
Weighs down upon my heart.

Sonnet

Most wonderful and strange it seems, that I
Who but a little time ago was tost
High on the waves of passion and of pain,
With aching heat and wildly throbbing brain,
Who peered into the darkness, deeming vain
All things there found if but One thing were lost,
Thus calm and still and silent here should lie,
Watching and waiting, waiting passively.

The dark has faded, and before mine eyes
Have long, grey flats expanded, dim and bare;
And through the changing guises all things wear
Inevitable Law I recognise:

Yet in my heart a hint of feeling lies
Which half a hope and half a despair.

To Clementina Black
More blest than was of old Diogenes,
I have not held my lantern up in vain.
Not mine, at least, this evil to complain:
"There is none honest among all of these."

Our hopes go down that sailed before the breeze;
Our creeds upon the rock are rent in twain;
Something it is, if at the last remain
One floating spar cast up by hungry seas.

The secret of our being, who can tell?
To praise the gods and Fate is not my part;
Evil I see, and pain ; within my heart
There is no voice that whispers: "All is well."

Yet fair are days in summer; and more fair
The growths of human goodness here and there.

The Old Poet
I will be glad because it is the Spring;
I will forget the winter in my heart
Dead hopes and withered promise; and will wring
A little joy from life ere life depart.

For spendthrift youth with passion-blinded eyes,
Stays not to see how woods and fields are bright;
He hears the phantom voices call, he flies
Upon the track of some unknown delight.

To him the tender glory of the May,
White wonder of the blossom, and the clear,
Soft green leaves that opened yesterday,
This only say: Forward, my friend, not here!

They breathe no other messages than this,
They have no other meaning for his heart;
Unto his troubled sense they tell of bliss,
Which make, themselves, of bliss the better part.

Yea, joy is near him, tho' he does not know;
Her unregarded shape is at his side,

Her unheard voice is whispering clear and low,
Whom, resting never, seeks he far and wide.

So once it was with us, my heart ! To-day
We will be glad because the leaves are green,
Because the fields are fair and soft with May,
Nor think on squandered springtimes that have been.

A Cross-Road Epitaph
When first the world grew dark to me
I call'd on God, yet came not he.
Whereon, as wearier wax'd my lot,
On Love I call'd, but Love came not.
When a worse evil did befall,
Death, on thee only did I call.

Straw in the Street
Straw in the street where I pass to-day
Dulls the sound of the wheels and feet.
'Tis for a failing life they lay
Straw in the street.

Here, where the pulses of London beat,
Someone strives with the Presence grey;
Ah, is it victory or defeat?

The hurrying people go their way,
Pause and jostle and pass and greet;
For life, for death, are they treading, say
Straw in the street?

The Village Garden
To E.M.S.
Here, where your garden fenced about and still is,
Here, where the unmoved summer air is sweet
With mixed delight of lavender and lilies,
Dreaming I linger in the noontide heat.

Of many summers are the trees recorders,
The turf a carpet many summers wove;
Old-fashioned blossoms cluster in the borders,
Love-in-a-mist and crimson-hearted clove.

All breathes of peace and sunshine in the present,

All tells of bygone peace and bygone sun,
Of fruitful years accomplished, budding, crescent,
Of gentle seasons passing one by one.

Fain would I bide, but ever in the distance
A ceaseless voice is sounding clear and low;
The city calls me with her old persistence,
The city calls me, I arise and go.

Of gentler souls this fragrant peace is guerdon;
For me, the roar and hurry of the town,
Wherein more lightly seems to press the burden
Of individual life that weighs me down.

I leave your garden to the happier comers
For whom its silent sweets are anodyne.
Shall I return? Who knows, in other summers
The peace my spirit longs for may be mine?

Contradictions

Now, even, I cannot think it true,
My friend, that there is no more you.
Almost as soon were no more I,
Which were, of course, absurdity!
Your place is bare, you are not seen,
Your grave, I'm told, is growing green;
And both for you and me, you know,
There's no Above and no Below.
That you are dead must be inferred,
And yet my thought rejects the word.

Between the Showers

Between the showers I went my way,
The glistening street was bright with flowers;
It seemed that March had turned to May
Between the showers.

Above the shining roofs and towers
The blue broke forth athwart the grey;
Birds carolled in their leafless bowers.

Hither and tither, swift and gay,
The people chased the changeful hours;
And you, you passed and smiled that day,
Between the showers.

Sinfonia Eroica

(To Sylvia.)

My Love, my Love, it was a day in June,
A mellow, drowsy, golden afternoon;
And all the eager people thronging came
To that great hall, drawn by the magic name
Of one, a high magician, who can raise
The spirits of the past and future days,
And draw the dreams from out the secret breast,
Giving them life and shape.
I, with the rest,
Sat there athirst, atremble for the sound;
And as my aimless glances wandered round,
Far off, across the hush'd, expectant throng,
I saw your face that fac'd mine.
Clear and strong
Rush'd forth the sound, a mighty mountain stream;
Across the clust'ring heads mine eyes did seem
By subtle forces drawn, your eyes to meet.

Then you, the melody, the summer heat,
Mingled in all my blood and made it wine.
Straight I forgot the world's great woe and mine;
My spirit's murky lead grew molten fire;
Despair itself was rapture.
Ever higher,
Stronger and clearer rose the mighty strain;
Then sudden fell; then all was still again,
And I sank back, quivering as one in pain.
Brief was the pause; then, 'mid a hush profound,
Slow on the waiting air swell'd forth a sound
So wondrous sweet that each man held his breath;
A measur'd, mystic melody of death.
Then back you lean'd your head, and I could note
The upward outline of your perfect throat;
And ever, as the music smote the air,
Mine eyes from far held fast your body fair.
And in that wondrous moment seem'd to fade
My life's great woe, and grow an empty shade
Which had not been, nor was not.
And I knew
Not which was sound, and which, O Love, was you.

A Greek Girl

I may not weep, not weep, and he is dead.
A weary, weary weight of tears unshed
Through the long day in my sad heart I bear;
The horrid sun with all unpitying glare
Shines down into the dreary weaving-room,
Where clangs the ceaseless clatter of the loom,
And ceaselessly deft maiden-fingers weave
The fine-wrought web; and I from morn till eve
Work with the rest, and when folk speak to me
I smile hard smiles; while still continually
The silly stream of maiden speech flows on:
And now at length they talk of him that's gone,
Lightly lamenting that he died so soon
Ah me! ere yet his life's sun stood at noon.
Some praise his eyes, some deem his body fair,
And some mislike the colour of his hair!
Sweet life, sweet shape, sweet eyes, and sweetest hair,
What form, what hue, save Love's own, did ye wear?
I may not weep, not weep, for very shame.

He loved me not. One summer's eve he came
To these our halls, my father's honoured guest,
And seeing me, saw not. If his lips had prest
My lips, but once, in love; his eyes had sent
One love-glance into mine, I had been content,
And deemed it great joy for one little life;
Nor envied other maids the crown of wife:
The long sure years, the merry children-band
Alas, alas, I never touched his hand!
And now my love is dead that loved not me.

Thrice-blest, thrice-crowned, of gods thrice-lovèd she
That other, fairer maid, who tombward brings
Her gold, shorn locks and piled-up offerings
Of fragrant fruits, rich wines, and spices rare,
And cakes with honey sweet, with saffron fair;
And who, unchecked by any thought of shame,
May weep her tears, and call upon his name,
With burning bosom prest to the cold ground,
Knowing, indeed, that all her life is crown'd,
Thrice-crowned, thrice honoured, with that love of his;
No dearer crown on earth is there, I wis.

While yet the sweet life lived, more light to bear
Was my heart's hunger; when the morn was fair,
And I with other maidens in a line
Passed singing through the city to the shrine,

Oft in the streets or crowded market-place
I caught swift glimpses of the dear-known face;
Or marked a stalwart shoulder in the throng;
Or heard stray speeches as we passed along,
In tones more dear to me than any song.
These, hoarded up with care, and kept apart,
Did serve as meat and drink my hungry heart.

And now for ever has my sweet love gone;
And weary, empty days I must drag on,
Till all the days of all my life be sped,
By no thought cheered, by no hope comforted.
For if indeed we meet among the shades,
How shall he know me from the other maids?
Me, that had died to save his body pain!

Alas, alas, such idle thoughts are vain!
O cruel, cruel sunlight, get thee gone!
O dear, dim shades of eve, come swiftly on!
That when quick lips, keen eyes, are closed in sleep,
Through the long night till dawn I then may weep.

To E.
The mountains in fantastic lines
Sweep, blue-white, to the sky, which shines
Blue as blue gems; athwart the pines
The lake gleams blue.

We three were here, three years gone by;
Our Poet, with fine-frenzied eye,
You, stepped in learned lore, and I,
A poet too.

Our Poet brought us books and flowers,
He read us Faust; he talked for hours
Philosophy (sad Schopenhauer's),
Beneath the trees:

And do you mind that sunny day,
When he, as on the sward he lay,
Told of Lassalle who bore away
The false Louise?

Thrice-favoured bard! to him alone
That green and snug retreat was shown,
Where to the vulgar herd unknown,

Our pens we plied.

(For, in those distant days, it seems,
We cherished sundry idle dreams,
And with our flowing foolscap reams
The Fates defied.)

And after, when the day was gone,
And the hushed, silver night came on,
He showed us where the glow-worm shone;
We stooped to see.

There, too, by yonder moon we swore
Platonic friendship o'er and o'er;
No folk, we deemed, had been before
So wise and free.

* * * * * * *

And do I sigh or smile to-day?
Dead love or dead ambition, say,
Which mourn we most? Not much we weigh
Platonic friends.

On you the sun is shining free;
Our Poet sleeps in Italy,
Beneath an alien sod; on me
The cloud descends.

A Minor Poet
Here is the phial; here I turn the key
Sharp in the lock. Click! there's no doubt it turned.
This is the third time; there is luck in threes
Queen Luck, that rules the world, befriend me now
And freely I'll forgive you many wrongs!
Just as the draught began to work, first time,
Tom Leigh, my friend (as friends go in the world),
Burst in, and drew the phial from my hand,
(Ah, Tom! ah, Tom! that was a sorry turn!)
And lectured me a lecture, all compact
Of neatest, newest phrases, freshly culled
From works of newest culture: "common good ;"
"The world's great harmonies;""must be content
With knowing God works all things for the best,
And Nature never stumbles." Then again,
"The common good," and still, "the common, good;"

And what a small thing was our joy or grief
When weigh'd with that of thousands. Gentle Tom,
But you might wag your philosophic tongue
From morn till eve, and still the thing's the same:
I am myself, as each man is himself
Feels his own pain, joys his own joy, and loves
With his own love, no other's. Friend, the world
Is but one man; one man is but the world.
And I am I, and you are Tom, that bleeds
When needles prick your flesh (mark, yours, not mine).
I must confess it; I can feel the pulse
A-beating at my heart, yet never knew
The throb of cosmic pulses. I lament
The death of youth's ideal in my heart;
And, to be honest, never yet rejoiced
In the world's progress, scarce, indeed, discerned;
(For still it seems that God's a Sisyphus
With the world for stone).
You shake your head. I'm base,
Ignoble? Who is noble, you or I?
I was not once thus? Ah, my friend, we are
As the Fates make us.
This time is the third;
The second time the flask fell from my hand,
Its drowsy juices spilt upon the board;
And there my face fell flat, and all the life
Crept from my limbs, and hand and foot were bound
With mighty chains, subtle, intangible;
While still the mind held to its wonted use,
Or rather grew intense and keen with dread,
An awful dread, I thought I was in Hell.
In Hell, in Hell ! Was ever Hell conceived
By mortal brain, by brain Divine devised,
Darker, more fraught with torment, than the world
For such as I? A creature maimed and marr'd
From very birth. A blot, a blur, a note
All out of tune in this world's instrument.
A base thing, yet not knowing to fulfil
Base functions. A high thing, yet all unmeet
For work that's high. A dweller on the earth,
Yet not content to dig with other men
Because of certain sudden sights and sounds
(Bars of broke music; furtive, fleeting glimpse
Of angel faces 'thwart the grating seen)
Perceived in Heaven. Yet when I approach
To catch the sound's completeness, to absorb
The faces' full perfection, Heaven's gate,

Which then had stood ajar, sudden falls to,
And I, a-shiver in the dark and cold,
Scarce hear afar the mocking tones of men:
"He would not dig, forsooth ; but he must strive
For higher fruits than what our tillage yields;
Behold what comes, my brothers, of vain pride!"
Why play with figures? trifle prettily
With this my grief which very simply's said,
"There is no place for me in all the world"?
The world's a rock, and I will beat no more
A breast of flesh and blood against a rock. . .
A stride across the planks for old time's sake.
Ah, bare, small room that I have sorrowed in;
Ay, and on sunny days, haply, rejoiced;
We know some things together, you and I!
Hold there, you rangèd row of books ! In vain
You beckon from your shelf. You've stood my friends
Where all things else were foes; yet now I'll turn
My back upon you, even as the world
Turns it on me. And yet, farewell, farewell!
You, lofty Shakespere, with the tattered leaves
And fathomless great heart, your binding's bruised
Yet did I love you less? Goethe, farewell;
Farewell, triumphant smile and tragic eyes,
And pitiless world-wisdom!

For all men
These two. And 'tis farewell with you, my friends,
More dear because more near: Theokritus;
Heine that stings and smiles; Prometheus' bard;
(I've grown too coarse for Shelley latterly:)
And one wild singer of to-day, whose song
Is all aflame with passionate bard's blood
Lash'd into foam by pain and the world's wrong.
At least, he has a voice to cry his pain;
For him, no silent writhing in the dark,
No muttering of mute lips, no straining out
Of a weak throat a-choke with pent-up sound,
A-throb with pent-up passion. . .
Ah, my sun!
That's you, then, at the window, looking in
To beam farewell on one who's loved you long
And very truly. Up, you creaking thing,
You squinting, cobwebbed casement!
So, at last,
I can drink in the sunlight. How it falls.
Across that endless sea of London roofs,

Weaving such golden wonders on the grey,
That almost, for the moment, we forget
The world of woe beneath them.
Underneath,
For all the sunset glory, Pain is king.

Yet, the sun's there, and very sweet withal;
And I'll not grumble that it's only sun,
But open wide my lips, thus, drink it in;
Turn up my face to the sweet evening sky
(What royal wealth of scarlet on the blue
So tender toned, you'd almost think it green)
And stretch my hands out, so to grasp it tight.
Ha, ha! 'tis sweet awhile to cheat the Fates,
And be as happy as another man.
The sun works in my veins like wine, like wine!
'Tis a fair world: if dark, indeed, with woe,
Yet having hope and hint of such a joy,
That a man, winning, well might turn aside,
Careless of Heaven....
O enough; I turn
From the sun's light, or haply I shall hope.
I have hoped enough; I would not hope again:
'Tis hope that is most cruel.
Tom, my friend,
You very sorry philosophic fool;
'Tis you, I think, that bid me be resign'd,
Trust, and be thankful.
Out on you! Resign'd?
I'm not resign'd, not patient, not school'd in
To take my starveling's portion and pretend
I'm grateful for it. I want all, all, all;
I've appetite for all. I want the best:
Love, beauty, sunlight, nameless joy of life.
There's too much patience in the world, I think.
We have grown base with crooking of the knee.
Mankind, say, God has bidden to a feast;
The board is spread, and groans with cates and drinks;
In troop the guests; each man with appetite
Keen-whetted with expectance.
In they troop,
Struggle for seats, jostle and push and seize.
What's this? what's this? There are not seats for all!
Some men must stand without the gates; and some
Must linger by the table, ill-supplied
With broken meats. One man gets meat for two,
The while another hungers. If I stand

Without the portals, seeing others eat
Where I had thought to satiate the pangs
Of mine own hunger; shall I then come forth
When all is done, and drink my Lord's good health
In my Lord's water? Shall I not rather turn
And curse him, curse him for a niggard host?
O, I have hungered, hungered, through the years,
Till appetite grows craving, then disease;
I am starved, wither'd, shrivelled.
Peace, O peace!
This rage is idle; what avails to curse
The nameless forces, the vast silences
That work in all things.
This time is the third,
I wrought before in heat, stung mad with pain,
Blind, scarcely understanding; now I know
What thing I do.
There was a woman once;
Deep eyes she had, white hands, a subtle smile,
Soft speaking tones: she did not break my heart,
Yet haply had her heart been otherwise
Mine had not now been broken. Yet, who knows?
My life was jarring discord from the first:
Tho' here and there brief hints of melody,
Of melody unutterable, clove the air.
From this bleak world, into the heart of night,
The dim, deep bosom of the universe,
I cast myself. I only crave for rest;
Too heavy is the load. I fling it down.

EPILOGUE.
We knocked and knocked; at last, burst in the door,
And found him as you know - the outstretched arms
Propping the hidden face. The sun had set,
And all the place was dim with lurking shade.
There was no written word to say farewell,
Or make more clear the deed.
I search'd and search'd;
The room held little: just a row of books
Much scrawl'd and noted; sketches on the wall,
Done rough in charcoal; the old instrument
(A violin, no Stradivarius)
He played so ill on; in the table drawer
Large schemes of undone work. Poems half-writ;
Wild drafts of symphonies; big plans of fugues;
Some scraps of writing in a woman's hand:
No more, the scattered pages of a tale,

A sorry tale that no man cared to read.
Alas, my friend, I lov'd him well, tho' he
Held me a cold and stagnant-blooded fool,
Because I am content to watch, and wait
With a calm mind the issue of all things.
Certain it is my blood's no turbid stream;
Yet, for all that, haply I understood
More than he ever deem'd; nor held so light
The poet in him. Nay, I sometimes doubt
If they have not, indeed, the better part
These poets, who get drunk with sun, and weep
Because the night or a woman's face is fair.
Meantime there is much talk about my friend.
The women say, of course, he died for love;
The men, for lack of gold, or cavilling
Of carping critics. I, Tom Leigh, his friend
I have no word at all to say of this.
Nay, I had deem'd him more philosopher;
For did he think by this one paltry deed
To cut the knot of circumstance, and snap
The chain which binds all being?

In a Minor Key
(AN ECHO FROM A LARGER LYRE.)

That was love that I had before
Years ago, when my heart was young;
Ev'ry smile was a gem you wore;
Ev'ry word was a sweet song sung.

You came - all my pulses burn'd and beat.
(O sweet wild throbs of an early day!)
You went - with the last dear sound of your feet
The light wax'd dim and the place grew grey.

And I us'd to pace with a stealthy tread
By a certain house which is under a hill;
A cottage stands near, wall'd white, roof'd red
Tall trees grow thick - I can see it still!

How I us'd to watch with a hope that was fear
For the least swift glimpse of your gown's dear fold!
(You wore blue gowns in those days, my dear
One light for summer, one dark for cold.)

Tears and verses I shed for you in show'rs;

I would have staked my soul for a kiss;
Tribute daily I brought you of flow'rs,
Rose, lily, your favourite eucharis.

There came a day we were doomed to part;
There's a queer, small gate at the foot of a slope:
We parted thereand I thought my heart
Had parted for ever from love and hope.

Is it love that I have to-day?
Love, that bloom'd early, has it bloom'd late
For me, that, clothed in my spirit's grey,
Sit in the stillness and stare at Fate?

Song nor sonnet for you I've penned,
Nor passionate paced by your home's wide wall
I have brought you never a flow'r, my friend,
Never a tear for your sake let fall.

And yet, and yet, ah, who understands?
We men and women are complex things!
A hundred tunes Fate's inexorable hands
May play on the sensitive soul-strings.

Webs of strange patterns we weave (each owns)
From colour and sound; and like unto these,
Soul has its tones and its semitones,
Mind has its major and minor keys.

Your face (men pass it without a word)
It haunts my dreams like an odd, sweet strain;
When your name is spoken my soul is stirr'd
In its deepest depths with a dull, dim pain.

I paced, in the damp grey mist, last night
In the streets (an hour) to see you pass:
Yet I do not think that I love you quite;
What's felt so finely 'twere coarse to class.

And yet, and yet, I scarce can tell why
(As I said, we are riddles and hard to read),
If the world went ill with you, and I
Could help with a hidden hand your need;

But, ere I could reach you where you lay,
Must strength and substance and honour spend;

Journey long journeys by night and day
Somehow, I think I should come, my friend!

In the Nower
To J. De P.
Deep in the grass outstretched I lie,
Motionless on the hill;
Above me is a cloudless sky,
Around me all is still:

There is no breath, no sound, no stir,
The drowsy peace to break:
I close my tired eyes, it were
So simple not to wake.

Ballade of a Special Edition
He comes; I hear him up the street
Bird of ill omen, flapping wide
The pinion of a printed sheet,
His hoarse note scares the eventide.
Of slaughter, theft, and suicide
He is the herald and the friend;
Now he vociferates with pride
A double murder in Mile End!

A hanging to his soul is sweet;
His gloating fancy's fain to bide
Where human-freighted vessels meet,
And misdirected trains collide.
With Shocking Accidents supplied,
He tramps the town from end to end.
How often have we heard it cried
A double murder in Mile End.

War loves he; victory or defeat,
So there be loss on either side.
His tale of horrors incomplete,
Imagination's aid is tried.
Since no distinguished man has died,
And since the Fates, relenting, send
No great catastrophe, he's spied
This double murder in Mile End.

Fiend, get thee gone! no more repeat
Those sounds which do mine ears offend.

It is apocryphal, you cheat,
Your double murder in Mile End.

In the Mile End Road
How like her! But 'tis she herself,
Comes up the crowded street,
How little did I think, the morn,
My only love to meet!

Whose else that motion and that mien?
Whose else that airy tread?
For one strange moment I forgot
My only love was dead.

A Prayer
Since that I may not have
Love on this side the grave,
Let me imagine Love.
Since not mine is the bliss
Of 'claspt hands and lips that kiss,'
Let me in dreams it prove.
What tho' as the years roll
No soul shall melt to my soul,
Let me conceive such thing;
Tho' never shall entwine
Loving arms around mine
Let dreams caresses bring.
To live, it is my doom
Lonely as in a tomb,
This cross on me was laid;
My God, I know not why;
Here in the dark I lie,
Lonely, yet not afraid.
It has seemed good to Thee
Still to withhold the key
Which opes the way to men;
I am shut in alone,
I make not any moan,
Thy ways are past my ken.
Yet grant me this, to find
The sweetness in my mind
Which I must still forego;
Great God which art above,
Grant me to image Love,
The bliss without the woe.

In the Night

Cruel? I think there never was a cheating
More cruel, thro' all the weary days than this!
This is no dream, my heart kept on repeating,
But sober certainty of waking bliss.

Dreams? O, I know their faces, goodly seeming,
Vaporous, whirled on many-coloured wings;
I have had dreams before, this is no dreaming,
But daylight gladness that the daylight brings.

What ails my love; what ails her? She is paling;
Faint grows her face, and slowly seems to fade!
I cannot clasp her, stretch out unavailing
My arms across the silence and the shade.

Epitaph. (On a Commonplace Person Who Died in Bed)

This is the end of him, here he lies:
The dust in his throat, the worm in his eyes,
The mould in his mouth, the turf on his breast;
This is the end of him, this is best.
He will never lie on his couch awake,
Wide-eyed, tearless, till dim daybreak.
Never again will he smile and smile
When his heart is breaking all the while.
He will never stretch out his hands in vain
Groping and groping, never again.
Never ask for bread, get a stone instead,
Never pretend that the stone is bread.
Never sway and sway 'twixt the false and true,
Weighing and noting the long hours through.
Never ache and ache with chok'd-up sighs;
This is the end of him, here he lies.

Impotens

If I were a woman of old,
What prayers I would pray for you, dear;
My pitiful tribute behold
Not a prayer, but a tear.

The pitiless order of things,
Whose laws we may change not nor break,

Alone I could face it, it wrings
My heart for your sake.

Ballade of an Omnibus
Some men to carriages aspire;
On some the costly hansoms wait;
Some seek a fly, on job or hire;
Some mount the trotting steed, elate.
I envy not the rich and great,
A wandering minstrel, poor and free,
I am contented with my fate
An omnibus suffices me.

In winter days of rain and mire
I find within a corner strait;
The 'busmen know me and my lyre
From Brompton to the Bull-and-Gate.
When summer comes, I mount in state
The topmost summit, whence I see
Crœsus look up, compassionate
An omnibus suffices me.

I mark, untroubled by desire,
Lucullus' phaeton and its freight.
The scene whereof I cannot tire,
The human tale of love and hate,
The city pageant, early and late
Unfolds itself, rolls by, to be
A pleasure deep and delicate.
An omnibus suffices me.

Princess, your splendour you require,
I, my simplicity; agree
Neither to rate lower nor higher.
An omnibus suffices me.

A Reminiscence
It is so long gone by, and yet
How clearly now I see it all!
The glimmer of your cigarette,
The little chamber, narrow and tall.

Perseus; your picture in its frame;
(How near they seem and yet how far!)
The blaze of kindled logs; the flame

Of tulips in a mighty jar.

Florence and spring-time: surely each
Glad things unto the spirit saith.
Why did you lead me in your speech
To these dark mysteries of death?

Felo de Se
With Apologies to Mr. Swinburne.

For repose I have sighed and have struggled ; have sigh'd and have
struggled in vain;
I am held in the Circle of Being and caught in the Circle of Pain.
I was wan and weary with life ; my sick soul yearned for death;
I was weary of women and war and the sea and the wind's wild breath;
I cull'd sweet poppies and crush'd them, the blood ran rich and red:
And I cast it in crystal chalice and drank of it till I was dead.
And the mould of the man was mute, pulseless in ev'ry part,
The long limbs lay on the sand with an eagle eating the heart.
Repose for the rotting head and peace for the putrid breast,
But for that which is 'I' indeed the gods have decreed no rest;
No rest but an endless aching, a sorrow which grows amain:
I am caught in the Circle of Being and held in the Circle of Pain.
Bitter indeed is Life, and bitter of Life the breath,
But give me Life and its ways and its men, if this be Death.
Wearied I once of the Sun and the voices which clamour'd around:
Give them me back, in the sightless depths there is neither light nor
sound.
Sick is my soul, and sad and feeble and faint as it felt
When (far, dim day) in the fair flesh-fane of the body it dwelt.
But then I could run to the shore, weeping and weary and weak;
See the waves' blue sheen and feel the breath of the breeze on my
cheek:
Could wail with the wailing wind; strike sharply the hands in despair;
Could shriek with the shrieking blast, grow frenzied and tear the hair;
Could fight fierce fights with the foe or clutch at a human hand;
And weary could lie at length on the soft, sweet, saffron sand. . .
I have neither a voice nor hands, nor any friend nor a foe;
I am I, just a Pulse of Pain, I am I, that is all I know.
For Life, and the sickness of Life, and Death and desire to die;
They have passed away like the smoke, here is nothing but Pain and I.

A Wall Flower
I lounge in the doorway and languish in vain
While Tom, Dick and Harry are dancing with Jane

My spirit rises to the music's beat;
There is a leaden fiend lurks in my feet!
To move unto your motion, Love, were sweet.

Somewhere, I think, some other where, not here,
In other ages, on another sphere,
I danced with you, and you with me, my dear.

In perfect motion did our bodies sway,
To perfect music that was heard alway;
Woe's me, that am so dull of foot to-day!

To move unto your motion, Love, were sweet;
My spirit rises to the music's beat
But, ah, the leaden demon in my feet!

Alma Mater
To-day in Florence all the air
Is soft with spring, with sunlight fair;
In the tall street gay folks are met;
Duomo and Tower gleam overhead,
Like jewels in the city set,
Fair-hued and many-faceted.
Against the old grey stones are piled
February violets, pale and sweet,
Whose scent of earth in woodland wild
Is wafted up and down the street.
The city's heart is glad; my own
Sits lightly on its bosom's throne.

Why is it that I see to-day,
Imaged as clear as in a dream,
A little city far away,
A churlish sky, a sluggish stream,
Tall clust'ring trees and gardens fair,
Dark birds that circle in the air,
Grey towers and fanes ; on either hand,
Stretches of wind-swept meadow-land?

Oh, who can sound the human breast?
And this strange truth must be confessed;
That city do I love the best
Wherein my heart was heaviest!

Lohengrin

Back to the mystic shore beyond the main
The mystic craft has sped, and left no trace.
Ah, nevermore may she behold his face,
Nor touch his hand, nor hear his voice again!
With hidden front she crouches; all in vain
The proffered balm. A vessel nears the place;
They bring her young, lost brother; see her strain
The new-found nursling in a close embrace.

God, we have lost Thee with much questioning.
In vain we seek Thy trace by sea and land,
And in Thine empty fanes where no men sing.
What shall we do through all the weary days?
Thus wail we and lament. Our eyes we raise,
And, lo, our Brother with an outstretched hand!

At a Dinner Party

With fruit and flowers the board is deckt,
The wine and laughter flow;
I'll not complain, could one expect
So dull a world to know?

You look across the fruit and flowers,
My glance your glances find.
It is our secret, only ours,
Since all the world is blind.

At Dawn

In the night I dreamed of you;
All the place was filled
With your presence; in my heart
The strife was stilled.

All night I have dreamed of you;
Now the morn is grey.
How shall I arise and face
The empty day?

Run to Death
A True Incident of Pre-Revolutionary French History.

Now the lovely autumn morning breathes its freshness in earth's face,
In the crowned castle courtyard the blithe horn proclaims the chase;
And the ladies on the terrace smile adieux with rosy lips

To the huntsmen disappearing down the cedar-shaded groves,
Wafting delicate aromas from their scented finger tips,
And the gallants wave in answer, with their gold-embroidered gloves.
On they rode, past bush and bramble, on they rode, past elm and oak;
And the hounds, with anxious nostril, sniffed the heather-scented air,
Till at last, within his stirrups, up Lord Gaston rose, and spoke
He, the boldest and the bravest of the wealthy nobles there:
'Friends,' quoth he, 'the time hangs heavy, for it is not as we thought,
And these woods, tho' fair and shady, will afford, I fear, no sport.
Shall we hence, then, worthy kinsmen, and desert the hunter's track
For the chateau, where the wine cup and the dice cup tempt us back?'
'Ay,' the nobles shout in chorus; 'Ay,' the powder'd lacquey cries;
Then they stop with eager movement, reining in quite suddenly;
Peering down with half contemptuous, half with wonder-opened eyes
At a 'something' which is crawling, with slow step, from tree to tree.
Is't some shadow phantom ghastly? No, a woman and a child,
Swarthy woman, with the 'gipsy' written clear upon her face;
Gazing round her with her wide eyes dark, and shadow-fringed, and wild,
With the cowed suspicious glances of a persecuted race.
Then they all, with unasked question, in each other's faces peer,
For a common thought has struck them, one their lips dare scarcely say,
Till Lord Gaston cries, impatient, 'Why regret the stately deer
When such sport as yonder offers? quick! unleash the dogs - away!'
Then they breath'd a shout of cheering, grey-haired man and stripling boy,
And the gipsy, roused to terror, stayed her step, and turned her head
Saw the faces of those huntsmen, lit with keenest cruel joy
Sent a cry of grief to Heaven, closer clasped her child, and fled!

O ye nobles of the palace! O ye gallant-hearted lords!
Who would stoop for Leila's kerchief, or for Clementina's gloves,
Who would rise up all indignant, with your shining sheathless swords,
At the breathing of dishonour to your languid lady loves!
O, I tell you, daring nobles, with your beauty-loving stare,
Who ne'er long the coy coquetting of the courtly dames withstood,
Tho' a woman be the lowest, and the basest, and least fair,
In your manliness forget not to respect her womanhood,
And thou, gipsy, that hast often the pursuer fled before,
That hast felt ere this the shadow of dark death upon thy brow,
That hast hid among the mountains, that hast roamed the forest o'er,
Bred to hiding, watching, fleeing, may thy speed avail thee now!

Still she flees, and ever fiercer tear the hungry hounds behind,
Still she flees, and ever faster follow there the huntsmen on,
Still she flees, her black hair streaming in a fury to the wind,
Still she flees, tho' all the glimmer of a happy hope is gone.
'Eh? what? baffled by a woman! Ah, sapristi! she can run!
Should she 'scape us, it would crown us with dishonour and disgrace;
It is time' (Lord Gaston shouted) 'such a paltry chase were done!'
And the fleeter grew her footsteps, so the hotter grew the chase
Ha! at last! the dogs are on her! will she struggle ere she dies?
See! she holds her child above her, all forgetful of her pain,
While a hundred thousand curses shoot out darkly from her eyes,

And a hundred thousand glances of the bitterest disdain.
Ha! the dogs are pressing closer! they have flung her to the ground;
Yet her proud lips never open with the dying sinner's cry
Till at last, unto the Heavens, just two fearful shrieks resound,
When the soul is all forgotten in the body's agony!
Let them rest there, child and mother, in the shadow of the oak,
On the tender mother-bosom of that earth from which they came.
As they slow rode back those huntsmen neither laughed, nor sang, nor spoke,
Hap, there lurked unowned within them throbbings of a secret shame.
But before the flow'ry terrace, where the ladies smiling sat,
With their graceful nothings trifling all the weary time away,
Low Lord Gaston bowed, and raising high his richly 'broider'd hat,
'Fairest ladies, give us welcome! 'Twas a famous hunt to-day.'

Twilight

So Mary died last night! To-day
The news has travelled here.
And Robert died at Michaelmas,
And Walter died last year.

I went at sunset up the lane,
I lingered by the stile;
I saw the dusky fields that stretched
Before me many a mile.

I leaned against the stile, and thought
Of her whose soul had fled
I knew that years on years must pass
Or e'er I should be dead.

Xantippe
(A Fragment)

What, have I waked again? I never thought
To see the rosy dawn, or ev'n this grey,
Dull, solemn stillness, ere the dawn has come.
The lamp burns low; low burns the lamp of life:
The still morn stays expectant, and my soul,
All weighted with a passive wonderment,
Waiteth and watcheth, waiteth for the dawn.
Come hither, maids; too soundly have ye slept
That should have watched me; nay, I would not chide
Oft have I chidden, yet I would not chide
In this last hour; now all should be at peace.
I have been dreaming in a troubled sleep
Of weary days I thought not to recall;
Of stormy days, whose storms are hushed long since;

Of gladsome days, of sunny days; alas!
In dreaming, all their sunshine seem'd so sad,
As though the current of the dark To-Be
Had flow'd, prophetic, through the happy hours.
And yet, full well, I know it was not thus;
I mind me sweetly of the summer days,
When, leaning from the lattice, I have caught
The fair, far glimpses of a shining sea;
And, nearer, of tall ships which thronged the bay,
And stood out blackly from a tender sky
All flecked with sulphur, azure, and bright gold;
And in the still, clear air have heard the hum
Of distant voices; and methinks there rose
No darker fount to mar or stain the joy
Which sprang ecstatic in my maiden breast
Than just those vague desires, those hopes and fears,
Those eager longings, strong, though undefined,
Whose very sadness makes them seem so sweet.
What cared I for the merry mockeries
Of other maidens sitting at the loom?
Or for sharp voices, bidding me return
To maiden labour? Were we not apart,
I and my high thoughts, and my golden dreams,
My soul which yearned for knowledge, for a tongue
That should proclaim the stately mysteries
Of this fair world, and of the holy gods?
Then followed days of sadness, as I grew
To learn my woman-mind had gone astray,
And I was sinning in those very thoughts
For maidens, mark, such are not woman's thoughts
(And yet, 'tis strange, the gods who fashion us
Have given us such promptings). . . .
Fled the years,
Till seventeen had found me tall and strong,
And fairer, runs it, than Athenian maids
Are wont to seem; I had not learnt it well
My lesson of dumb patience and I stood
At Life's great threshold with a beating heart,
And soul resolved to conquer and attain. . . .
Once, walking 'thwart the crowded market place,
With other maidens, bearing in the twigs
White doves for Aphrodite's sacrifice,
I saw him, all ungainly and uncouth,
Yet many gathered round to hear his words,
Tall youths and stranger-maidens, Sokrates
I saw his face and marked it, half with awe,
Half with a quick repulsion at the shape. . . .

The richest gem lies hidden furthest down,
And is the dearer for the weary search;
We grasp the shining shells which strew the shore,
Yet swift we fling them from us; but the gem
We keep for aye and cherish. So a soul,
Found after weary searching in the flesh
Which half repelled our senses, is more dear,
For that same seeking, than the sunny mind
Which lavish Nature marks with thousand hints
Upon a brow of beauty. We are prone
To overweigh such subtle hints, then deem,
In after disappointment, we are fooled. . .
And when, at length, my father told me all,
That I should wed me with great Sokrates,
I, foolish, wept to see at once cast down
The maiden image of a future love,
Where perfect body matched the perfect soul.
But slowly, softly did I cease to weep;
Slowly I 'gan to mark the magic flash
Leap to the eyes, to watch the sudden smile
Break round the mouth, and linger in the eyes;
To listen for the voice's lightest tone
Great voice, whose cunning modulations seemed
Like to the notes of some sweet instrument.
So did I reach and strain, until at last
I caught the soul athwart the grosser flesh.
Again of thee, sweet Hope, my spirit dreamed!
I, guided by his wisdom and his love,
Led by his words, and counselled by his care,
Should lift the shrouding veil from things which be,
And at the flowing fountain of his soul
Refresh my thirsting spirit. . .
And indeed,
In those long days which followed that strange day
When rites and song, and sacrifice and flow'rs,
Proclaimed that we were wedded, did I learn,
In sooth, a-many lessons; bitter ones
Which sorrow taught me, and not love inspired,
Which deeper knowledge of my kind impressed
With dark insistence on reluctant brain;
But that great wisdom, deeper, which dispels
Narrowed conclusions of a half-grown mind,
And sees athwart the littleness of life
Nature's divineness and her harmony,
Was never poor Xantippe's. . .
I would pause
And would recall no more, no more of life,

Than just the incomplete, imperfect dream
Of early summers, with their light and shade,
Their blossom-hopes, whose fruit was never ripe;
But something strong within me, some sad chord
Which loudly echoes to the later life,
Me to unfold the after-misery
Urges with plaintive wailing in my heart.
Yet, maidens, mark; I would not that ye thought
I blame my lord departed, for he meant
No evil, so I take it, to his wife.
'Twas only that the high philosopher,
Pregnant with noble theories and great thoughts,
Deigned not to stoop to touch so slight a thing
As the fine fabric of a woman's brain
So subtle as a passionate woman's soul.
I think, if he had stooped a little, and cared,
I might have risen nearer to his height,
And not lain shattered, neither fit for use
As goodly household vessel, nor for that
Far finer thing which I had hoped to be. . .
Death, holding high his retrospective lamp,
Shows me those first, far years of wedded life,
Ere I had learnt to grasp the barren shape
Of what the Fates had destined for my life.
Then, as all youthful spirits are, was I
Wholly incredulous that Nature meant
So little, who had promised me so much.
At first I fought my fate with gentle words,
With high endeavours after greater things;
Striving to win the soul of Sokrates,
Like some slight bird, who sings her burning love
To human master, till at length she finds
Her tender language wholly misconceived,
And that same hand whose kind caress she sought,
With fingers flippant flings the careless corn. . .
I do remember how, one summer's eve,
He, seated in an arbour's leafy shade,
Had bade me bring fresh wine-skins. . .
As I stood
Ling'ring upon the threshold, half concealed
By tender foliage, and my spirit light
With draughts of sunny weather, did I mark
An instant, the gay group before mine eyes.
Deepest in shade, and facing where I stood,
Sat Plato, with his calm face and low brows
Which met above the narrow Grecian eyes,
The pale, thin lips just parted to the smile,

Which dimpled that smooth olive of his cheek.
His head a little bent, sat Sokrates,
With one swart finger raised admonishing,
And on the air were borne his changing tones.
Low lounging at his feet, one fair arm thrown
Around his knee (the other, high in air
Brandish'd a brazen amphor, which yet rained
Bright drops of ruby on the golden locks
And temples with their fillets of the vine),
Lay Alkibiades the beautiful.
And thus, with solemn tone, spake Sokrates:
' This fair Aspasia, which our Perikles
Hath brought from realms afar, and set on high
In our Athenian city, hath a mind,
I doubt not, of a strength beyond her race;
And makes employ of it, beyond the way
Of women nobly gifted : woman's frail
Her body rarely stands the test of soul;
She grows intoxicate with knowledge; throws
The laws of custom, order, 'neath her feet,
Feasting at life's great banquet with wide throat.'
Then sudden, stepping from my leafy screen,
Holding the swelling wine-skin o'er my head,
With breast that heaved, and eyes and cheeks aflame,
Lit by a fury and a thought, I spake:
' By all great powers around us! can it be
That we poor women are empirical?
That gods who fashioned us did strive to make
Beings too fine, too subtly delicate,
With sense that thrilled response to ev'ry touch
Of nature's and their task is not complete?
That they have sent their half-completed work
To bleed and quiver here upon the earth?
To bleed and quiver, and to weep and weep,
To beat its soul against the marble walls
Of men's cold hearts, and then at last to sin!'
I ceased, the first hot passion stayed and stemmed
And frighted by the silence: I could see,
Framed by the arbour foliage, which the sun
In setting softly gilded with rich gold,
Those upturned faces, and those placid limbs;
Saw Plato's narrow eyes and niggard mouth,
Which half did smile and half did criticise,
One hand held up, the shapely fingers framed
To gesture of entreaty 'Hush, I pray,
Do not disturb her; let us hear the rest;
Follow her mood, for here's another phase

Of your black-browed Xantippe. . .'
Then I saw
Young Alkibiades, with laughing lips
And half-shut eyes, contemptuous shrugging up
Soft, snowy shoulders, till he brought the gold
Of flowing ringlets round about his breasts.
But Sokrates, all slow and solemnly,
Raised, calm, his face to mine, and sudden spake:
' I thank thee for the wisdom which thy lips
Have thus let fall among us : prythee tell
From what high source, from what philosophies
Didst cull the sapient notion of thy words?'
Then stood I straight and silent for a breath,
Dumb, crushed with all that weight of cold contempt;
But swiftly in my bosom there uprose
A sudden flame, a merciful fury sent
To save me; with both angry hands I flung
The skin upon the marble, where it lay
Spouting red rills and fountains on the white;
Then, all unheeding faces, voices, eyes,
I fled across the threshold, hair unbound
White garment stained to redness, beating heart
Flooded with all the flowing tide of hopes
Which once had gushed out golden, now sent back
Swift to their sources, never more to rise. . .
I think I could have borne the weary life,
The narrow life within the narrow walls,
If he had loved me; but he kept his love
For this Athenian city and her sons;
And, haply, for some stranger-woman, bold
With freedom, thought, and glib philosophy. . .
Ah me ! the long, long weeping through the nights,
The weary watching for the pale-eyed dawn
Which only brought fresh grieving : then I grew
Fiercer, and cursed from out my inmost heart
The Fates which marked me an Athenian maid.
Then faded that vain fury ; hope died out;
A huge despair was stealing on my soul,
A sort of fierce acceptance of my fate,
He wished a household vessel well! 'twas good,
For he should have it! He should have no more
The yearning treasure of a woman's love,
But just the baser treasure which he sought.
I called my maidens, ordered out the loom,
And spun unceasing from the morn till eve;
Watching all keenly over warp and woof,
Weighing the white wool with a jealous hand.

I spun until, methinks, I spun away
The soul from out my body, the high thoughts
From out my spirit; till at last I grew
As ye have known me, eye exact to mark
The texture of the spinning; ear all keen
For aimless talking when the moon is up,
And ye should be a-sleeping; tongue to cut
With quick incision, 'thwart the merry words
Of idle maidens. . .
Only yesterday
My hands did cease from spinning; I have wrought
My dreary duties, patient till the last.
The gods reward me! Nay, I will not tell
The after years of sorrow; wretched strife
With grimmest foes, sad Want and Poverty;
Nor yet the time of horror, when they bore
My husband from the threshold; nay, nor when
The subtle weed had wrought its deadly work.
Alas! alas! I was not there to soothe
The last great moment; never any thought
Of her that loved him, save at least the charge,
All earthly, that her body should not starve. . .
You weep, you weep; I would not that ye wept;
Such tears are idle; with the young, such grief
Soon grows to gratulation, as, 'her love
Was withered by misfortune; mine shall grow
All nurtured by the loving,' or, 'her life
Was wrecked and shattered, mine shall smoothly sail.'
Enough, enough. In vain, in vain, in vain!
The gods forgive me! Sorely have I sinned
In all my life. A fairer fate befall
You all that stand there. . .
Ha! the dawn has come;
I see a rosy glimmer, nay ! it grows dark;
Why stand ye so in silence? throw it wide,
The casement, quick; why tarry?give me air
O fling it wide, I say, and give me light!

Last Words
These blossoms that I bring,
This song that here I sing,
These tears that now I shed,
I give unto the dead.

There is no more to be done,
Nothing beneath the sun,

All the long ages through,
Nothing by me for you.

The tale is told to the end;
This, ev'n, I may not know
If we were friend and friend,
If we were foe and foe.

All's done with utterly,
All's done with. Death to me
Was ever Death indeed;
To me no kindly creed

Consolatory was given.
You were of earth, not Heaven. . .
This dreary day, things seem
Vain shadows in a dream,

Or some strange, pictured show;
And mine own tears that flow,
My hidden tears that fall,
The vainest of them all.

The Promise of Sleep
Put the sweet thoughts from out thy mind,
The dreams from out thy breast;
No joy for thee but thou shalt find
Thy rest

All day I could not work for woe,
I could not work nor rest;
The trouble drove me to and fro,
Like a leaf on the storm's breast.

Night came and saw my sorrow cease;
Sleep in the chamber stole;
Peace crept about my limbs, and peace
Fell on my stormy soul.

And now I think of only this,
How I again may woo
The gentle sleep who promises
That death is gentle too.

The End of the Day

To B. T.

Dead-tired, dog-tired, as the vivid day
Fails and slackens and fades away.
The sky that was so blue before
With sudden clouds is shrouded o'er.
Swiftly, stilly the mists uprise,
Till blurred and grey the landscape lies.

All day we have plied the oar; all day
Eager and keen have said our say
On life and death, on love and art,
On good or ill at Nature's heart.
Now, grown so tired, we scarce can lift
The lazy oars, but onward drift.
And the silence is only stirred
Here and there by a broken word.

O, sweeter far than strain and stress
Is the slow, creeping weariness.
And better far than thought I find
The drowsy blankness of the mind.
More than all joys of soul or sense
Is this divine indifference;
Where grief a shadow grows to be,
And peace a possibility.

Magdalen
All things I can endure, save one.
The bare, blank room where is no sun;
The parcelled hours; the pallet hard;
The dreary faces here within;
The outer women's cold regard;
The Pastor's iterated "sin";
These things could I endure, and count
No overstrain'd, unjust amount;
No undue payment for such bliss
Yea, all things bear, save only this:
That you, who knew what thing would be,
Have wrought this evil unto me.
It is so strange to think on still
That you, that you should do me ill!
Not as one ignorant or blind,
But seeing clearly in your mind
How this must be which now has been,

Nothing aghast at what was seen.
Now that the tale is told and done,
It is so strange to think upon.
You were so tender with me, too!
One summer's night a cold blast blew,
Closer about my throat you drew
That half-slipt shawl of dusky blue.
And once my hand, on summer's morn,
I stretched to pluck a rose; a thorn
Struck through the flesh and made it bleed
(A little drop of blood indeed!)
Pale grew your cheek you stoopt and bound
Your handkerchief about the wound;
Your voice came with a broken sound;
With the deep breath your breast was riven;
I wonder, did God laugh in Heaven?

How strange, that you should work my woe!
How strange! I wonder, do you know
How gladly, gladly I had died
(And life was very sweet that tide)
To save you from the least, light ill?
How gladly I had borne your pain.
With one great pulse we seem'd to thrill,
Nay, but we thrill'd with pulses twain.

Even if one had told me this,
"A poison lurks within your kiss,
Gall that shall turn to night his day:"
Thereon I straight had turned away
Ay, tho' my heart had crack'd with pain
And never kiss'd your lips again.

At night, or when the daylight nears,
I hear the other women weep;
My own heart's anguish lies too deep
For the soft rain and pain of tears.
I think my heart has turn'd to stone,
A dull, dead weight that hurts my breast;
Here, on my pallet-bed alone,
I keep apart from all the rest.
Wide-eyed I lie upon my bed,
I often cannot sleep all night;
The future and the past are dead,
There is no thought can bring delight.
All night I lie and think and think;
If my heart were not made of stone,

But flesh and blood, it needs must shrink
Before such thoughts. Was ever known
A woman with a heart of stone?

The doctor says that I shall die.
It may be so, yet what care I?
Endless reposing from the strife?
Death do I trust no more than life.
For one thing is like one arrayed,
And there is neither false nor true;
But in a hideous masquerade
All things dance on, the ages through.
And good is evil, evil good;
Nothing is known or understood
Save only Pain. I have no faith
In God, or Devil, Life or Death.

The doctor says that I shall die.
You, that I knew in days gone by,
I fain would see your face once more,
Con well its features o'er and o'er;
And touch your hand and feel your kiss,
Look in your eyes and tell you this:
That all is done, that I am free;
That you, through all eternity,
Have neither part nor lot in me.

The Last Judgment
With beating heart and lagging feet,
Lord, I approach the Judgment-seat.
All bring hither the fruits of toil,
Measures of wheat and measures of oil;

Gold and jewels and precious wine;
No hands bare like these hands of mine.
The treasure I have nor weighs nor gleams:
Lord, I can bring you only dreams.

In days of spring, when my blood ran high,
I lay in the grass and looked at the sky,
And dreamed that my love lay by my side
My love was false, and then she died.

All the heat of the summer through,
I dreamed she lived, that her heart was true
Throughout the hours of the day I slept,

But woke in the night, at times, and wept.

The nights and days, they went and came,
I lay in shadow and dreamed of fame;
And heard men passing the lonely place,
Who marked me not and my hidden face.

My strength waxed faint, my hair grew grey;
Nothing but dreams by night and day.
Some men sicken, with wine and food;
I starved on dreams, and found them good.

This is the tale I have to tell
Show the fellow the way to hell.

To a Dead Poet
I knew not if to laugh or weep;
They sat and talked of you
"'Twas here he sat; 'twas this he said!
'Twas that he used to do.

"Here is the book wherein he read,
The room wherein he dwelt;
And he" (they said) "was such a man,
Such things he thought and felt."

I sat and sat, I did not stir;
They talked and talked away.
I was as mute as any stone,
I had no word to say.

They talked and talked; like to a stone
My heart grew in my breast
I, who had never seen your face
Perhaps I knew you best.

To Death
(From Lenau.)

If within my heart there's mould,
If the flame of Poesy
And the flame of Love grow cold,
Slay my body utterly.

Swiftly, pause not nor delay;

Let not my life's field be spread
With the ash of feelings dead,
Let thy singer soar away.

Printed in Great Britain
by Amazon

51660565R00036